Camping

Cookbook

Camping Cookbook with Easy Outdoor Campfire recipes for Everyone. Dutch Oven, Cast Iron and Other Methods Included!

John Carter

Disclaimer Notice:

Please note the information contained within this document is for educational and entertainment purposes only. All effort has been executed to present accurate, up to date, and reliable, complete information. No warranties of any kind are declared or implied. Readers acknowledge that the author is not engaging in the rendering of legal, financial, medical or professional advice. The content within this book has been derived from various sources. Please consult a licensed professional before attempting any techniques outlined in this book.

By reading this document, the reader agrees that under no circumstances is the author responsible for any losses, direct or indirect, which are incurred as a result of the use of information contained within this document, including, but not limited to, errors, omissions, or inaccuracies.

Table of Content

Electric Smoker

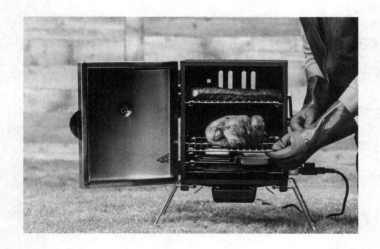

Breakfast

Smoked Lemony-Garlic Artichokes

Preparation time: 15 minutes

Cooking time: 20 minutes

Servings: 54

Ingredients:

- 4 artichokes
- 4 minced garlic cloves
- 3 tbsps. Lemon juice
- ½ c. virgin olive oil
- 2 parsley sprigs
- Sea salt

Directions:

1. Put a large pot on your stove with a metal steaming basket inside. Boil water just to the bottom of the basket.

2. Cut the artichoke tail and take out the toughest leaves. Clip the pointy ends off of the outermost leaves.

3. Cut the artichokes in half lengthwise. Remove the hairy choke in the center. Put the halves, stem side down, in the steamer basket. Reduce the heat to a rolling simmer.

4. On the pot, cover and steam for about 20 to 25 minutes, until the inside of the artichoke is tender. Prepare a dressing: place in a mortar the garlic, lemon juice, olive oil, parsley, and salt.

5. Take away the basket and let the artichokes come to room temperature. Preheat your smoker to 200°F.

6. Place the artichokes in aluminum foil packets and brush garlic mixture all over the artichokes. Smoke the artichoke halves within 1 hour. Serve hot.

Nutrition: Calories: 140 Carbs: 2g Fat: 8g Protein: 16g

Simple But Delicious Fish Recipe

Preparation Time: 45 minutes

Cooking Time: 10 minutes

Servings: 4 - 6

Ingredients:

*   4 lbs. fish cut it into pieces (portion size)

*   1 tablespoon minced Garlic

*   1/3 cup of Olive oil

*   1 cup of Soy Sauce

*   Basil, chopped

*   2 Lemons, the juice

Directions:

1. Preheat the grill to 350F with closed lid.

2. Combine the ingredients in a bowl. Stir to combine.

Marinade the fish for 45 min.

3. Grill the fish until it reaches 145F internal temperature.

4. Serve with your favorite side dish and enjoy!

Nutrition: Calories: 153 Protein: 25g Carbohydrates: 1g

Fiber: 0.3g Fat: 4g

Smoked Squash Casserole

Preparation time: 15 minutes

Cooking time: 40 minutes

Servings: 2

Ingredients:

- 2½ lbs. yellow squash
- 2 tbsps. parsley flakes
- 2 eggs, beaten
- 1 medium yellow onion
- 1 sleeve saltine crackers
- 1 package Velveeta cheese
- ½ cup Alouette Sundried Tomato
- Basil cheese spread
- ¼ cup Alouette Garlic and Herb cheese spread
- ¼ cup mayonnaise
- ¾ tsp. hot sauce
- ¼ tsp. Cajun seasoning
- ½ cup butter
- ¼ tsp. salt
- ¼ tsp. black pepper

Directions:

1.   Preheat the electric smoker to 250 F. Combine squash and onion in a large saucepan and add water to cover. Boil on medium heat until tender.

2.   Drain and to this hot mixture, add Velveeta cheese, Alouette cheese, mayonnaise, parsley flakes, hot sauce, Cajun seasoning, salt, and pepper to taste. Stir all together well.

3.   Cool a little, add eggs, and stir until mixed. Melt butter in a saucepan. Add crushed crackers to the butter and stir well. Combine ½ cup of butter-cracker mix with the squash mixture. Stir thoroughly.

4.   Pour into a disposable aluminum foil pan, then top the squash with the remaining butter and crackers. Cover the pan tightly with aluminum foil.

5.   Put on the lower rack of the smoker and cook for 1 hr. Put one small handful of prepared wood chips in the wood tray for the best result, use hickory.

6.   After an hour, remove the foil from the casserole and cook for another 15 minutes.

Nutrition: Calories: 65 Carbs: 8g Fat: 1g Protein: 5g

Smoked Baked Beans

Preparation time: 15 minutes

Cooking time: 2-3 hours

Servings: 6-8

Ingredients:

- 6 slices bacon, cut widthwise into 1/4" pieces

- 1 large yellow/white onion, finely chopped

- 1 red/green bell pepper, chopped into small bite-size

- 2 cloves garlic, minced

- 3 15-ounce cans of Great Northern beans, drained & rinsed

- 1/3 cup packed dark brown sugar

- 1/3 cup ketchup

- 1/4 cup dark molasses

- 2-1/2 tbsp apple cider vinegar, preferably unfiltered

- 2 tbsp Worcestershire sauce

- 1-1/2 tbsp Dijon mustard

- Salt

- ground black pepper

- 3/4 cup dark beer/water (not added all at once)

Directions:

1.   In a heavy oven-proof pot, sauté the bacon over medium heat within 5 minutes. Drain off all except for 2 tablespoons of the bacon fat.

2.   Put the onion, bell pepper, plus garlic and cook within 5 minutes. Mix in the beans, sugar, ketchup, molasses, vinegar, Worcestershire sauce, plus mustard.

3.   Put salt plus pepper to taste. Mix in some of the beer or water, then reserve the rest for adding later, if needed.

4.   Warm your smoker to 225°F with the top vent open, then put water to half full in the bottom bowl. Put wood chips on the side tray.

5.   Put the pot on a rack inside your smoker, uncovered. Smoke within 2 to 3 hours.

6.   Mix occasionally and put more beer or water as needed if the beans are drying out too much. Remember to replenish the wood chips and water as needed, approximately every 60 minutes.

Nutrition: Calories: 150 Carbs: 29g Fat: 1g Protein: 7g

Lunch

Chipotle Garlic Shrimp

Preparation time: 1 hour & 15 minutes

Cooking time: 45 minutes

Servings: 6

Ingredients:

- 3 tablespoons chopped fresh cilantro leaves

- 2 tablespoons olive oil

- 2 tablespoons lime juice

- 4 garlic cloves (minced)

- 2 teaspoons canned chipotle chili peppers plus 2

teaspoons sauce from the can

- Kosher salt

- ground black pepper,

- 2 pounds jumbo shrimp (tails on, peeled, deveined)

- Barbecue sauce, as desired, for dipping

Directions:

1.   For the marinade, mix cilantro, olive oil, lime juice, garlic cloves, and chipotle chili peppers with sauce and season to taste with salt and pepper in a large mixing bowl.

2.   Put shrimp to marinade and toss to coat. Cover the bowl and refrigerate within 30 minutes to 1 hour. Place oak wood chips in the electric smoker's wood tray and preheat the smoker to 250°F.

3.   Remove shrimp from marinade and place on the smoker grate. Smoke shrimp within 45 minutes. Serve shrimp immediately with barbecue sauce as desired, and enjoy!

Nutrition: Calories: 178 Fat: 5g Protein: 28g Carbs: 7g

Smoked Trout

Preparation time: 2-8 hours & 20 minutes

Cooking time: 1 hour

Servings: 6

Ingredients:

- 3 cups water, plus more as needed

- 1/4 cup white sugar

- 1/4 cup brown sugar

- 1/4 cup salt

- 1 tablespoon lemon juice

- 2 teaspoons garlic powder

- 2 teaspoons chili powder

- 4 skin-on boneless trout (about 2 pounds)

- 2 tablespoons vegetable oil

Directions:

1. For the brine, mix water, sugars, salt, lemon juice, garlic powder, and chili powder in a large glass baking dish.

2. Add trout to the baking dish and pour more water over trout as necessary to submerge. Cover baking dish and refrigerate for 2 to 8 hours.

3.　　Place hickory wood chips in the electric smoker's wood tray and preheat the smoker to 225°F. Rinse trout with cold water, pat dry and brush with vegetable oil.

4.　　Place trout skin-side down on smoker grate and smoke until flaky, about 1 hour. Serve trout immediately and enjoy!

Nutrition: Calories: 287 Fat: 13g Protein: 40g Carbs: 0g

Dinner

Elegant Lamb Chops

Preparation Time: 15 minutes

Cooking Time: 30 Minutes

Servings: 4

Ingredients:

- 4 lamb shoulder chops

- 4 C. buttermilk

- 1 C. cold water

- ¼ C. kosher salt

- 2 tbsp. olive oil

- 1 tbsp. Texas-style rub

Directions:

1. In a large bowl, add buttermilk, water and salt and stir until salt is dissolved.

2. Add chops and coat with mixture evenly.

3. Refrigerate for at least 4 hours.

4. Remove the chops from bowl and rinse under cold running water.

5. Coat the chops with olive oil and then sprinkle with rub evenly.

6. Set the temperature of Grill to 240 degrees F and preheat with closed lid for 15 minutes, using charcoal.

7. Arrange the chops onto grill and cook for about 25-30 minutes or until desired doneness.

8. Meanwhile, preheat the broiler of oven. Grease a broiler pan.

9. Remove the chops from grill and place onto the prepared broiler pan.

10. Transfer the broiler pan into the oven and broil for about 3-5 minutes or until browned.

11. Remove the chops from oven and serve hot.

Nutrition: Calories per serving: 414; Carbohydrates: 11.7g; Protein: 5.6g; Fat: 22.7g; Sugar: 11.7g; Sodium: 7000mg; Fiber: 0g

Spicy & Tangy Lamb Shoulder

Preparation time; 30 minutes

Cooking Time: 5¾ Hours

Servings: 6

Ingredients:

- 1 (5-lb.) bone-in lamb shoulder, trimmed

- 3-4 tbsp. Moroccan seasoning

- 2 tbsp. olive oil

- 1 C. water

- ¼ C. apple cider vinegar

Directions:

1. Set the temperature of Grill to 275 degrees F and preheat with closed lid for 15 minutes, using charcoal.

2. Coat the lamb shoulder with oil evenly and then rub with Moroccan seasoning generously.

3. Place the lamb shoulder onto the grill and cook for about 45 minutes.

4. In a food-safe spray bottle, mix together vinegar and water.

5. Spray the lamb shoulder with vinegar mixture evenly.

6.   Cook for about 4-5 hours, spraying with vinegar mixture after every 20 minutes.

7.   Remove the lamb shoulder from grill and place onto a cutting board for about 20 minutes before slicing.

8.   With a sharp knife, cut the lamb shoulder in desired sized slices and serve.

Nutrition: Calories per serving: 563; Carbohydrates: 3.1g; Protein: 77.4g; Fat: 25.2g; Sugar: 1.4g; Sodium: 1192mg; Fiber: 0g

Smoked Lamb Meatballs

Preparation Time: 30 minutes

Cooking Time: 1 Hour

Servings: 20

Ingredients:

- 1 lb. lamb shoulder, ground

- 3 garlic cloves, finely diced

- 3 tbsp. shallot, diced

- 1 tbsp. salt

- 1 egg

- 1/2 tbsp. pepper

- 1/2 tbsp. cumin

- 1/2 tbsp. smoked paprika

- 1/4 tbsp. red pepper flakes

- 1/4 tbsp. cinnamon

- 1/4 cup panko breadcrumbs

Directions:

1. Set you're to 250F.

2. Combine all the ingredients in a small bowl then mix thoroughly using your hands.

3.   Form golf ball-sized meatballs and place them in a baking sheet.

4.   Place the baking sheet in the smoker and smoke until the internal temperature reaches 160F.

5.   Remove the meatballs from the smoker and serve when hot.

Nutrition : Calories 93, Total fat 5.9g, Saturated fat 2.5g, Total carbs 4.8g, Net carbs 4.5g Protein 5g, Sugars 0.3g, Fiber 0.3g, Sodium 174.1mg, Potassium 82.8mg

SNACKS

Ancho-Dusted Jícama Sticks with Lime

Preparation Time: 15 minutes

Cooking Time: 30 minutes

Servings: 8

Ingredients:

- 1 2-pound jícama, trimmed and peeled

- 2 tablespoons good-quality olive oil

- 2 teaspoons ancho chile powder

- Salt

- 1 lime, cut into wedges

Directions:

1. Warm the gas grill for medium-high direct cooking at 350 F. Make sure the grates are clean.

2. Cut the jícama into ½-inch slices, then oiled the slices on both sides with the olive oil. Put the slices on your grill directly over the fire.

3.   Cook, turning once, within 7 to 10 minutes per side. Transfer the jícama to a cutting board and cut the slices into ½-inch-wide sticks.

4.   Put on a platter, then sprinkle with the ancho powder and salt to taste, turning them to coat evenly. Squeeze the lime wedges over them, again turning to coat evenly, and serve.

Nutrition: Calories: 49 Fats: 0.1 g Carbohydrates: 12 g Proteins: 1 g

DESSERTS

Smoked Banana Pudding

Preparation time: 10 minutes

Cooking time: 30 minutes

Servings: 6

Ingredients:

- 4 bananas

- ¼ cup brown sugar

- ¼ cup melted butter

- Sprinkle of cinnamon

- 10 egg yolks

- 1-quart whole milk

- ½ cup white sugar

- 1 cup heavy cream

- Splash of light rum

- 1 teaspoon pure vanilla extract

- 2 tablespoons unflavored powdered gelatin

- 1 cup crushed nilla wafers (for serving)

Directions:

1.	Leave the peel on, and cut bananas in half. Preheat your smoker to 200-degrees with the wood chips in the container.

2.	When the smoker is ready, put the banana halves on the top rack. Smoke for just 30 minutes. Remove from the smoker and unpeel.

3.	Mix brown sugar, melted butter, and cinnamon. Put bananas in an oven-safe skillet and pour over brown sugar/butter mixture. Broil for just 5 minutes or so, until caramelizing.

4.	In a blender, mix smoked bananas with yolks, milk, and white sugar. When smooth, add in 1 cup cream, rum, and vanilla, and mix. Move this puree into a saucepan.

5.	Whisk in the gelatin. Heat on medium-high until pudding is 135-degrees. Cook at this temp for 5 minutes, then strain. Chill in the fridge until firm, then serve with crushed nilla wafers on top!

Nutrition: Calories: 587 Protein: 15.4g Carbs: 63.5g Fat: 32g

Smoked Pineapple

Preparation time: 15 minutes

Cooking time: 2 hours & 30 minutes

Servings: 8-10

Ingredients:

• 1 whole sliced pineapple

• Generous sprinkle of brown sugar

• Vanilla ice cream (for serving)

Directions:

1. Preheat your smoker to 250-degrees with the wood chips. Put pineapple in a foil pan. Sprinkle with brown sugar. Smoke for 2 ½ hours. Serve with vanilla ice cream!

Nutrition: Calories: 127 Protein: 1.7g Carbs: 23.5g Fat: 3.6g

BBQ

BREAKFAST

New Mexican Salsa Verde

Preparation Time: 5 Minutes

Cooking Time: 15 Minutes

Servings: 1 Cup

Ingredients:

- cloves garlic (leave the skins on),

- skewered on a wooden toothpick or small bamboo skewer

- 1 cup roasted New Mexican green chiles or Anaheim chiles cut into ¼-inch strips (8 to 10 chiles

- 2 tablespoons chopped fresh cilantro

- 2 teaspoons fresh lime juice, or more to

- taste

- ½ teaspoon ground cumin

- ½ teaspoon dried oregano

- Coarse salt (kosher or sea) and freshly

- ground black pepper

Directions:

1.   Preheat the griddle to high. When ready to cook, lightly oil the griddle surface. Place the burgers on the hot griddle. The burgers will be done after cooking 4 to 6 minutes. Put the garlic cloves until they are lightly browned and tender, 2 to 3 minutes per side (4 to 6 minutes in all). Scrape any really burnt skin off the garlic. Place the garlic, chile strips, cilantro, lime juice, cumin, oregano, and 4 tablespoons of water in a blender and purée until smooth, scraping down the sides of the blender with a spatula.

2.   Transfer the salsa to a saucepan and bring to a gentle simmer over medium heat. Let simmer until thick and flavorful, 5 to 8 minutes, stirring with a wooden spoon. The salsa should be thick (roughly the consistency of heavy cream) but pourable; add more water as needed. Taste for seasoning, adding more lime juice as necessary and salt and pepper to taste; the salsa should be highly seasoned.

Nutrition: Calories: 214; Fat: 16g; Protein:36g; Fiber:2g

Tzatziki Lamb Burgers

Preparation Time: 5 Minutes

Cooking Time: 12 Minutes

Servings: 5

Ingredients:

- 1½ pounds boneless lamb shoulder or leg or good-quality ground lamb

- 1 tablespoon chopped fresh oregano

- 1 teaspoon salt

- 1 teaspoon black pepper

- 1 tablespoon minced garlic

- ½ cup Greek yogurt

- 1 tablespoon olive oil, plus more for brushing

- 1 tablespoon red wine vinegar

- 2 tablespoons crumbled feta cheese

- 4 or 5 ciabatta rolls, split, or 8–10 slider buns (like potato or dinner rolls)

- Thinly sliced cucumbers for serving

Directions:

1.   Put the lamb, oregano, salt, pepper, and garlic in a food processor and pulse until coarsely ground—finer than chopped, but not much. (If you're using preground meat, put it in a bowl with the seasonings and work them together gently with your hands.) Take a bit of the mixture and fry it up to taste for seasoning; adjust if necessary. Handling the meat as little as possible to avoid compressing it, shape the mixture lightly into 4 or 5 burgers or 8 to 10 sliders. Refrigerate the burgers until you're ready to griddle; if you make them several hours in advance, cover with plastic wrap.

2.   Whisk the yogurt, oil, and vinegar together in a small bowl until smooth. Stir in the feta. Taste and adjust the seasoning with salt and pepper.

3.   Bring the griddle to high heat. When the griddle is hot, place the burgers and cook for 11 minutes.

4.   Transfer the burgers to a plate. Brush the cut sides of the rolls lightly with oil and toast directly over the griddle, 1 to 2 minutes. Top with a burger, then several slices of cucumber, a dollop of the sauce, and the other half of the roll. Serve with the remaining sauce on the side.

Nutrition: Calories: 134; Fat: 21g; Protein:36g; Fiber:2g

LUNCH

Wood Pellet Pulled Pork

Preparation Time: 15 Minutes

Cooking Time: 12 Hours

Servings: 12

Ingredients:

- 8 lb. pork shoulder roast, bone-in

- BBQ rub

- 3 cups apple cider, dry hard

Directions:

1. Fire up the wood pellet grill and set it to smoke.

2. Meanwhile, rub the pork with BBQ rub on all sides, then place it on the grill grates. Cook for 5 hours, flipping it every 1 hour.

3. Increase the heat to 225°F and continue cooking for 3 hours directly on the grate.

4. Transfer the pork to a foil pan and place the apple cider at the bottom of the pan.

5.   Cook until the internal temperature reaches 200°F then remove it from the grill. Wrap the pork loosely with foil, then let it rest for 1 hour.

6.   Remove the fat layer and use forks to shred it.

7.   Serve and enjoy.

Nutrition: Calories 912 Total fat 65g Saturated fat 24g Total Carbs 7g Net Carbs 7g Protein 70g Sugar 6g Fiber 0g Sodium: 208mg

Lovable Pork Belly

Preparation Time: 15 Minutes

Cooking Time: 4 Hours and 30 Minutes

Servings: 4

Ingredients:

- 5 pounds of pork belly
- 1 cup dry rub
- Three tablespoons olive oil

For Sauce

- Two tablespoons honey
- Three tablespoons butter
- 1 cup BBQ sauce

Directions:

1. Take your drip pan and add water. Cover with aluminum foil.

2. Pre-heat your smoker to 250 degrees F

3. Add pork cubes, dry rub, olive oil into a bowl and mix well

4. Use water fill water pan halfway through and place it over drip pan.

5.   Add wood chips to the side tray

6.   Transfer pork cubes to your smoker and smoke for 3 hours (covered)

7.   Remove pork cubes from the smoker and transfer to foil pan, add honey, butter, BBQ sauce, and stir

8.   Cover the pan with foil and move back to a smoker, smoke for 90 minutes more

9.   Remove foil and smoke for 15 minutes more until the sauce thickens

10.   Serve and enjoy!

Nutrition: Calories: 1164 Fat: 68g Carbohydrates: 12g Protein: 104g

Wood Pellet Togarashi Pork Tenderloin

Preparation Time: 5 Minutes

Cooking Time: 25 Minutes

Servings: 6

Ingredients:

- 1 Pork tenderloin

- 1/2tbsp kosher salt

- 1/4 cup Togarashi seasoning

Directions:

1. Cut any excess silver skin from the pork and sprinkle with salt to taste. Rub generously with the togarashi seasoning

2. Place in a preheated oven at 400°F for 25 minutes or until the internal temperature reaches 145°F.

3. Remove from the grill and let rest for 10 minutes before slicing and serving.

4. Enjoy.

Nutrition: Calories 390 Total fat 13g Saturated fat 6g Total Carbs 4g Net Carbs 1g Protein 33g Sugar 0g

Fiber 3g Sodium: 66mg

DINNER

Smoked Honey - Garlic Pork Chops

Preparation Time: 15 minutes

Cooking Time: 1 hour

Servings: 4

Ingredients:

- 1/4 cup of lemon juice freshly squeezed

- 1/4 cup honey (preferably a darker honey)

- 3 cloves garlic, minced

- 2 Tbs soy sauce (or tamari sauce)

- Salt and pepper to taste

- 24 ounces center-cut pork chops boneless

Directions:

1. Combine honey, lemon juice, soy sauce, garlic and the salt and pepper in a bowl.

2. Place pork in a container and pour marinade over pork.

3. Cover and marinate in a fridge overnight.

4. In a meantime, heat remaining marinade in a small saucepan over medium heat to simmer.

5.   Transfer pork chops on a serving plate, pour with the marinade and serve hot.

Nutrition: Calories: 301.5 Carbs: 17g Fat: 6.5g Fiber: 0.2g Protein: 41g

Smoked Pork Burgers

Preparation Time: 30 minutes

Cooking Time: 1 hour 15 minutes

Servings: 4

Ingredients:

- 2 lbs. ground pork

- 1/2 of onion finely chopped

- 2 Tbsp fresh sage, chopped

- 1 tsp garlic powder

- 1 tsp cayenne pepper

- salt and pepper to taste

Directions:

1. Start the pellet grill (recommended hickory pellet) on SMOKE with the lid open until the fire is established. Set the temperature to 225 degree F and preheat, lid closed, for 10 to 15 minutes.

2. In a bowl, combine ground pork with all remaining ingredients.

3. Use your hands to mix thoroughly. Form mixture into 8 evenly burgers.

4.   Place the hamburgers on the racks.

5.   Smoke the burgers for 60 to 90 minutes until they
reach an internal temperature of 150 to 160°F.

6.   Serve hot.

Nutrition: Calories: 588.7 Carbs: 1g Fat: 48.2g Fiber: 0.5g

Protein: 38.4g

SNACKS

Simplest Grilled Asparagus

Preparation Time: 0 minutes

Cooking Time: 25 minutes

Servings: 4

Ingredients:

- 1½–2 pounds asparagus

- 1–2 tablespoons good-quality olive oil or melted butter

- Salt

Directions:

1.   Start the coals or heat a gas grill for direct hot cooking. Make sure the grates are clean.

2.   Cut the tough bottoms from the asparagus. If they're thick, trim the ends with a vegetable peeler. Toss with the oil and sprinkle with salt.

3.   Put the asparagus on the grill directly over the fire, perpendicular to the grates, so they don't fall through. Close the lid and cook, turning once, until the thick part of the stalks

can barely be pierced with a skewer or thin knife, 5 to 10 minutes' total. Transfer to a platter and serve.

Nutrition: Calories: 225 Fats: 20.6 g Cholesterol: 0 mg

Carbohydrates: 9.1 g Fiber: 4.2 g Sugars: 0 g Proteins: 4.6 g

DESSERTS

Kale Chips

Preparation Time: 30 Minutes

Cooking Time: 20 Minutes

Servings: 4

Ingredients:

- 4 cups kale leaves
- Olive oil
- Salt to taste

Directions:

1. Drizzle kale with oil and sprinkle it with salt.
2. Set the Traeger wood pellet grill to 250 degrees F.
3. Preheat it for 15 minutes while the lid is closed.
4. Add the kale leaves to a baking pan.
5. Place the pan on the grill.
6. Cook the kale for 20 minutes or until crispy.

Nutrition: Calories 118 Total fat 7.6g Total carbs 10.8g Protein 5.4g, Sugars 3.7g Fiber 2.5g, Sodium 3500mg Potassium 536mg

CAMPING

BREAKFAST

Lemon Chicken in Foil Packet

Preparation Time: 5 Minutes

Cooking Time: 25 Minutes

Servings: 4

Ingredients:

- 4 chicken fillets

- 3 tablespoon melted butter

- 1 garlic, minced

- 1-1/2 teaspoon dried Italian seasoning

- Salt and pepper to taste

- 1 lemon, sliced

Directions:

1. Turn on your wood pellet grill.

2. Keep the lid open while burning for 5 minutes.

3. Preheat it to 450 degrees F.

4. Add the chicken fillet on top of foil sheets.

5.   In a bowl, mix the butter, garlic, seasoning, salt and

pepper.

6.   Brush the chicken with this mixture.

7.   Put the lemon slices on top.

8.   Wrap the chicken with the foil.

9.   Grill each side for 7 to 10 minutes per side.

Nutrition: Calories 935 Total fat 53g Saturated fat 15g Protein

107g Sodium 320mg

Asian Wings

Preparation Time: 30 Minutes

Cooking Time: 3 Hours

Servings: 6

Ingredients:

- 1 teaspoon honey

- 1 teaspoon soy sauce

- 2 teaspoon rice vinegar

- 1/2 cup hoisin sauce

- 2 teaspoon sesame oil

- 1 teaspoon ginger, minced

- 1 teaspoon garlic, minced

- 1 teaspoon green onion, chopped

- 1 cup hot water

- 2 lb. chicken wings

Directions:

1.   Combine all the sauce fixings in a large bowl. Mix well.

2.   Transfer 1/3 of the sauce to another bowl and refrigerate.

3.   Add the chicken wings to the remaining sauce.

4.   Cover and refrigerate for 2 hours.

5.   Turn on your wood pellet grill.

6.   Set it to 300 degrees F.

7.   Add the wings to a grilling basket.

8.   Cook for 1 hour.

9.   Heat the reserved sauce in a pan.

10.   Bring to a boil and then simmer for 10 minutes.

11.   Brush the chicken with the remaining sauce.

12.   Grill for another 10 minutes.

13.   Let rest for 5 minutes before serving.

Nutrition: Calories 935 Total fat 53g Saturated fat 15g Protein 107g Sodium 320mg

LUNCH

Turkey Legs

Preparation Time: 10 Minutes

Cooking Time: 5 Hours

Servings: 4

Ingredients:

- 4 turkey legs
- For the Brine:
- ½ cup curing salt
- 1 tablespoon whole black peppercorns
- 1 cup BBQ rub
- ½ cup brown sugar
- 2 bay leaves
- 2 teaspoons liquid smoke
- 16 cups of warm water
- 4 cups ice
- 8 cups of cold water

Directions:

1.   Prepare the brine and for this, take a large stockpot, place it over high heat, pour warm water in it, add peppercorn, bay leaves, and liquid smoke, stir in salt, sugar, and BBQ rub and bring it to a boil.

2.   Remove pot from heat, bring it to room temperature, then pour in cold water, add ice cubes and let the brine chill in the refrigerator.

3.   Then add turkey legs in it, submerge them completely, and let soak for 24 hours in the refrigerator.

4.   After 24 hours, remove turkey legs from the brine, rinse well and pat dry with paper towels.

5.   When ready to cook, switch on the grill, fill the grill hopper with hickory flavored wood pellets, power the grill on by using the control panel, select 'smoke' on the temperature dial, or set the temperature to 250 degrees F and let it preheat for a minimum of 15 minutes.

6.   When the grill has preheated, open the lid, place turkey legs on the grill grate, shut the grill, and smoke for 5 hours until nicely browned and the internal temperature reaches 165 degrees F. Serve immediately.

Nutrition: Calories: 416 Fat: 13.3 g Carbs: 0 g Protein: 69.8 g

Turkey Breast

Preparation Time: 12 Hours

Cooking Time: 8 Hours

Servings: 6

Ingredients:

For the Brine:

- 2 pounds turkey breast, deboned

- 2 tablespoons ground black pepper

- ¼ cup salt

- 1 cup brown sugar

- 4 cups cold water

For the BBQ Rub:

- 2 tablespoons dried onions

- 2 tablespoons garlic powder

- ¼ cup paprika

- 2 tablespoons ground black pepper

- 1 tablespoon salt

- 2 tablespoons brown sugar

- 2 tablespoons red chili powder

- 1 tablespoon cayenne pepper

- 2 tablespoons sugar

- 2 tablespoons ground cumin

Directions:

1.   Prepare the brine and for this, take a large bowl, add salt, black pepper, and sugar in it, pour in water, and stir until sugar has dissolved.

2.   Place turkey breast in it, submerge it completely and let it soak for a minimum of 12 hours in the refrigerator.

3.   Meanwhile, prepare the BBQ rub and for this, take a small bowl, place all of its ingredients in it and then stir until combined, set aside until required.

4.   Then remove turkey breast from the brine and season well with the prepared BBQ rub.

5.   When ready to cook, switch on the grill, fill the grill hopper with apple-flavored wood pellets, power the grill on by using the control panel, select 'smoke' on the temperature dial, or set the temperature to 180 degrees F and let it preheat for a minimum of 15 minutes.

6. When the grill has preheated, open the lid, place turkey breast on the grill grate, shut the grill, change the smoking temperature to 225 degrees F, and smoke for 8 hours until the internal temperature reaches 160 degrees F.

7. When done, transfer turkey to a cutting board, let it rest for 10 minutes, then cut it into slices and serve.

Nutrition: Calories: 250 Fat: 5 g Carbs: 31 g Protein: 18 g

Herb Roasted Turkey

Preparation Time: 15 Minutes

Cooking Time: 3 Hours 30 Minutes

Servings: 12

Ingredients:

- 14 pounds turkey, cleaned
- 2 tablespoons chopped mixed herbs
- Pork and poultry rub as needed
- ¼ teaspoon ground black pepper
- 3 tablespoons butter, unsalted, melted
- 8 tablespoons butter, unsalted, softened
- 2 cups chicken broth

Directions:

1.   Clean the turkey by removing the giblets, wash it inside out, pat dry with paper towels, then place it on a roasting pan and tuck the turkey wings by tiring with butcher's string.

2.   Switch on the grill, fill the grill hopper with hickory flavored wood pellets, power the grill on by using the control panel, select 'smoke' on the temperature dial, or set the

temperature to 325 degrees F and let it preheat for a minimum of 15 minutes.

3.   Meanwhile, prepared herb butter and for this, take a small bowl, place the softened butter in it, add black pepper and mixed herbs and beat until fluffy.

4.   Place some of the prepared herb butter underneath the skin of turkey by using a handle of a wooden spoon, and massage the skin to distribute butter evenly.

5.   Then rub the exterior of the turkey with melted butter, season with pork and poultry rub, and pour the broth in the roasting pan.

6.   When the grill has preheated, open the lid, place roasting pan containing turkey on the grill grate, shut the grill and smoke for 3 hours and 30 minutes until the internal temperature reaches 165 degrees F and the top has turned golden brown.

7.   When done, transfer turkey to a cutting board, let it rest for 30 minutes, then carve it into slices and serve.

Nutrition: Calories: 154.6 Fat: 3.1 g Carbs: 8.4 g Protein: 28.8 g

DINNER

Lightly Spiced Smoked Turkey

Preparation time: 30 minutes

Cooking Time: 6 Hours

Servings: 10

Ingredients:

- Whole Turkey - 1 (10-lbs., 4.5-kgs)

- Vegetable oil – ¼ cup

- The Injection

- Beer – ¾ cup, at room temperature

- Butter – ½ cup, melted

- Garlic – 6 cloves

- Worcestershire sauce – 2 ½ tablespoons

- Creole seasoning – 1 ½ tablespoons

- Hot sauce – 1 ½ tablespoons

- Salt – 1 ½ tablespoons

- Cayenne pepper – ½ teaspoon

- The Rub

- Paprika – 1 ½ teaspoons

- Garlic powder – 1 teaspoon

- Onion powder – 1 teaspoon

- Thyme – ¾ teaspoon

- Oregano – ¼ teaspoon

- Cumin – ¼ teaspoon

- Salt – ½ teaspoon

- Black pepper – 1 teaspoon

- The Fire

- Preheat the smoker an hour prior to smoking.

- Use charcoal and hickory wood chips for smoking.

Directions:

1.   Preheat a smoker to 225°F (107°C) with charcoal and hickory wood chips. Wait until the smoker is ready.

2.   Place garlic, Worcestershire sauce, Creole seasoning, hot sauce, salt, and cayenne pepper in a blender.

3.   Pour beer and melted butter into the blender then blend until smooth.

4.   Inject all sides of the turkey—give space about 1-inch. Set aside.

5. After that, make the rub by combining paprika with garlic powder, onion powder, thyme, oregano, cumin, salt, and black pepper. Mix well.

6. Rub the turkey with the spice mixture then lightly brush with vegetable oil.

7. When the smoker is ready, place the seasoned turkey in the smoker.

8. Smoke the turkey for 6 hours or until the internal temperature has reached 160°F (71°C).

9. Remove the turkey from the smoker then let it sit for a few minutes.

10. Carve the smoked turkey then serve.

11. Enjoy!

Nutrition: Carbohydrates: 27 g Protein: 19 g Sodium: 65 mg Cholesterol: 49 mg

Tempting Tarragon Turkey Breasts

Preparation Time: 20 Minutes (Marinating Time: Overnight)

Cooking Time: 3½ to 4 hours

Servings: 4 to 5

Ingredients:

- For the marinade

- ¾ cup heavy (whipping) cream

- ¼ cup Dijon mustard

- ¼ cup dry white wine

- 2 tablespoons olive oil

- ½ cup chopped scallions, both white and green parts, divided

- 3 tablespoons fresh tarragon, finely chopped

- 6 garlic cloves, coarsely chopped

- 1 teaspoon salt

- 1 teaspoon freshly ground black pepper

- For the turkey:

- (6- to 7-pound) bone-in turkey breast

- ¼ cup (½ stick) unsalted butter, melted

Directions:

1. To make the marinade

2. In a large bowl, whisk together the cream, mustard, wine, and olive oil until blended.

3. Stir in ¼ cup of scallions and the tarragon, garlic, salt, and pepper.

4. Rub the marinade all over the turkey breast and under the skin. Cover and refrigerate overnight.

5. To make the turkey

6. Following the manufacturer's specific start-up procedure, preheat the smoker to 250°F, and add apple or mesquite wood.

7. Remove the turkey from the refrigerator and place it directly on the smoker rack. Do not rinse it.

8. Smoke the turkey for 3½ to 4 hours (about 30 minutes per pound), basting it with the butter twice during smoking, until the skin is browned and the internal temperature registers 165°F.

9. Remove the turkey from the heat and let it rest for 10 minutes.

10. Sprinkle with the remaining scallions before serving.

Nutrition: Calories: 165 cal Fat: 14g Carbohydrates: 0.5g Fiber: 0 g Protein: 15.2g

Hot Smoked Turkey with Jelly Glaze

Preparation time: 30 minutes

Cooking Time: 6 Hours

Servings: 1

Ingredients:

- Whole Turkey - 1 (10-lbs., 4.5-kgs)

- The Rub

- Olive oil – ½ cup

- Salt – 3 tablespoons

- Pepper – 2 tablespoons

- The Glaze

- Hot pepper jelly – ¾ cup

- Rice vinegar – 3 tablespoons

- Red pepper flakes – ¼ cup

- The Fire

- Preheat the smoker an hour prior to smoking.

- Use charcoal and hickory wood chips for smoking.

Directions:

1.   Preheat a smoker to 225°F (107°C) with charcoal and hickory wood chips. Wait until the smoker is ready.

2. Cut the excess fat of the turkey then brush all sides of the turkey with olive oil,

3. Sprinkle salt and pepper over the turkey then place it in the smoker.

4. Smoke the turkey for 6 hours or until the internal temperature has reached 160°F (71°C).

5. Meanwhile, combine hot pepper jelly with rice vinegar and red pepper flakes then mix well.

6. After 6 hours, brush the smoked turkey with the hot pepper jelly mixture then return to the smoker.

7. Smoke for about 20 minutes then remove from the smoker.

8. Let the smoked turkey warm for a few minutes then cut into slices.

9. Arrange on a serving dish then serve.

10. Enjoy!

Nutrition: Carbohydrates: 27 g Protein: 19 g Sodium: 65 mg Cholesterol: 49 mg

SNACKS

Cocoa-Rubbed Steak for Two

Preparation Time: 50 minutes

Cooking Time: 50 hours

Servings: 4

Smoke Temperature: 135Farenheit

Preferred Wood Pellet: Apricot or Alder

Ingredients:

- 2 whole rib-eye roast, trimmed

- 1 cup Trigger Coffee Rub

- 1/4 cup cocoa powder

Directions:

1. Cut the roast into 21/2-inch-thick steaks. Set aside 2 steaks and freeze for later use.

2. Mix the Trigger Coffee rub and cocoa powder in a bowl. Season the steaks lightly with the rub mixture. Reserve the remaining rub mixture for later use.

3. Set the Trigger and preheat, lid closed for 15 minutes.

4. Season the steaks with Trigger Beef Rub.

5.   Arrange the steaks directly on the grill and smoke for 60 minutes.

6.   Remove the steaks from the grill and set aside to rest.

7.   Take out the steaks and cool for 5 minutes before serving.

Nutrition: Calories: 764 Fat: 55g Carbohydrates: 2g Protein: 63g

DESSERTS

S'mores Dip

Preparation Time: 10 minutes

Cooking Time: 25 minutes

Servings: 8

Ingredients:

- 12 ounces semisweet chocolate chips

- ¼ cup milk

- 2 tablespoons melted salted butter

- 16 ounces marshmallows

- Apple wedges

- Graham crackers

Directions:

1. Add wood pellets to your smoker and follow your cooker's startup procedure. Preheat your smoker, with your lid closed, until it reaches 450.

2. Put a cast iron skillet on your grill and add in the milk and melted butter. Stir together for a minute.

3.   Once it has heated up, top with the chocolate chips, making sure it makes a single layer. Place the marshmallows on top, standing them on their end and covering the chocolate.

4.   Cover, and let it smoke for five to seven minutes. The marshmallows should be toasted lightly.

5.   Take the skillet off the heat and serve with apple wedges and graham crackers.

Nutrition: Calories: 216.7 Protein: 2.7g Carbs: 41g Fat: 4.7g

DUTCH

BREAKFAST

Broccoli Crisps

Preparation Time: 10 Minutes

Cooking Time: 12 Minutes

Servings: 4

Ingredients:

- Large chopped broccoli head,

- Salt, 1 tsp.

- Olive oil, 2 tbsps.

- Black pepper, 1 tsp.

Directions:

1. Set the dutch oven to heat up to 3600f.

2. Using a bowl, add and toss the broccoli florets with olive oil, salt, and black pepper.

3. Add the broccoli florets and cook it for 12 minutes, then shake after 6 minutes.

4. Carefully remove it from your dutch oven and allow it to cool off.

5. Serve and enjoy!

Nutrition: Calories: 120 Fat: 19g Protein: 5g Carbs: 3g

Mac and Cheese Balls

Preparation Time: 20 Minutes

Cooking Time: 25 Minutes

Servings: 6

Ingredients:

- ½ shredded pound mozzarella cheese

- 2 eggs

- 3 cup seasoned panko breadcrumbs

- Salt

- 2 tbsps. All-purpose flour

- 1 lb. Grated cheddar cheese

- 1 lb. Elbow macaroni

- 2 cup heated cream

- Pepper

- 2 tbsps. Unsalted butter

- 2 tbsps. Egg wash

- ½ lb. Shredded parmesan cheese

Directions:

1.   Prepare the macaroni in relation to the directions on the package.

2.   Rinse with cold water and drain. Transfer to a bowl and set aside.

3.   Melt butter in a saucepan over medium flame. Add flour and whisk for a couple of minutes. Stir the heated cream until there are no more lumps. Cook until thick. Remove from the stove. Stir in the cheeses until melted. Season with salt and pepper.

4.   Top the cheese mixture onto the cooked macaroni. Gently fold until combined. Transfer to a shallow pan and refrigerate for 2 hours.

5.   Use your hands to form meatball-sized balls from the mixture. Arrange them in a tray lined with wax paper. Freeze overnight.

6.   Prepare the egg wash by combining 2 tbsps. Of cream and eggs in a shallow bowl.

7.   Dip the frozen mac and cheese balls in the egg wash and coat them with panko breadcrumbs. Gently press to make the coating stick.

8.   Arrange them in the cooking basket. Cook for 8 minutes at 400 degrees.

Nutrition: Calories: 907 Fat: 423g Carbs: 874g Protein: 499g

Maple Syrup Bacon

Preparation Time: 5 Minutes

Cooking Time: 10 Minutes

Servings: 2

Ingredients:

- Maple syrup.

- Thick bacon slices, 1

Directions:

1. Preheat your dutch oven to 400°f.

2. Place the bacon on the flat surface and brush with the maple syrup.

3. Move to the dutch oven to cook for 10 minutes.

4. Serve and enjoy!

Nutrition: Calories: 91 Carbs: 0gProtein: 8g Fat: 2g

LUNCH

Bacon-Wrapped Shrimp and Jalapeño

Preparation Time: 20 Minutes

Cooking Time: 13 Minutes

Servings: 8

Ingredients:

- 24 large shrimp, peeled and deveined, about ¾ pound (340 g)
- Five tablespoons barbecue sauce, divided
- 12 strips bacon, cut in half
- 24 small pickled jalapeño slices

Directions:

1. Toss together the shrimp and three tablespoons of the barbecue sauce. Let stand for 15 minutes. Soak 24 wooden toothpicks in water for 10 minutes. Wrap 1-piece bacon around the shrimp and jalapeño slice, then secure with a toothpick.

2. Preheat the dutch oven oven to 350°F (177°C).

3.   Position the shrimp in the dutch oven basket, spacing them ½ inch apart.

4.   Place the dutch oven basket onto the baking pan.

5.   Slide into Rack Position 2, select Air Fry, and set time to 10 minutes.

6.   Turn shrimp over with tongs and air fry for 3 minutes more, or until bacon is golden brown and shrimp are cooked through.

7.   Brush with the remaining barbecue sauce and serve.

Nutrition: Calories: 246 Protein: 14.4g Fiber: 0.6 g Net Carbohydrates: 2.0 g Fat: 17.9 g Sodium: 625 Mg Carbohydrates: 2.6 g

Breaded Artichoke Hearts

Preparation Time: 5 Minutes

Cooking Time: 8 Minutes

Servings: 14

Ingredients:

- 14 whole artichoke hearts, packed in water
- One egg
- ½ cup all-purpose flour
- 1/3 cup panko bread crumbs
- One teaspoon Italian seasoning

Directions:

1. Preheat the dutch oven oven to 380°F (193°C)

2. Squeeze excess water from the artichoke hearts and place them on paper towels to dry.

3. In a small bowl, beat the egg.

4. In another small bowl, place the flour.

5. In a third small bowl, blend the bread crumbs and Italian seasoning, and stir.

6. Spritz the dutch oven basket by means of cooking spray.

7.   Drench the artichoke hearts in the flour, then the egg, and then the bread crumb mixture.

8.   Place the breaded artichoke hearts in the dutch oven basket. Spray them with cooking spray.

9.   Place the dutch oven basket onto the baking pan.

10.   Slide into Rack Position 2, select Air Fry, and set time to 8 minutes. You may wait until the artichoke hearts have browned and are crisp. Flip once halfway through the cooking time.

11.   Let cool for 5 minutes before serving.

Nutrition: Calories: 149 Fat: 1g Carbohydrates: 5g Protein: 30g

DINNER

Simple Beef Sirloin Roast

Preparation Time: 10 Minutes

Cooking Time: 50 Minutes

Servings: 8

Ingredients:

•	2½ pounds sirloin roast

•	Salt and ground black pepper, as required

Directions:

1.	Rub the roast with salt and black pepper generously.

2.	Insert the rotisserie rod through the roast.

3.	Insert the rotisserie forks, one on each rod's side, to secure the rod to the chicken.

4.	Select "Roast" and then adjust the temperature to 350 degrees F.

5.	Set the timer for 50 minutes and press the "Start."

6.	When the display shows "Add Food," press the red lever down.

7.	Weight the left side of the rod into the Vortex.

8. Now, turn the rod's left side into the groove along the metal bar so it will not move.

9. Then, close the door and touch "Rotate." Press the red lever to release the rod when cooking time is complete.

10. Remove from the Vortex.

11. Place the roast onto a platter for about 10 minutes before slicing.

12. With a sharp knife, cut the roast into desired sized slices and serve.

Nutrition: Calories 201 Fat 8.8 g Carbs 0 g Protein 28.9 g

Simple Beef Patties

Preparation Time: 10 Minutes

Cooking Time: 13 Minutes

Servings: 4

Ingredients:

- 1 lb. ground beef
- ½ tsp garlic powder
- ¼ tsp onion powder
- Pepper
- Salt

Directions:

1. Preheat the instant vortex dutch oven oven to 400 F.

2. Add ground meat, garlic powder, onion powder, pepper, and salt into the mixing bowl and mix until well combined.

3. Make even shape patties from meat mixture and arrange on dutch oven pan.

4. Place pan in instant vortex dutch oven oven.

5. Cook patties for 10 minutes Turn patties after 5 minutes

6. Serve and enjoy.

Nutrition: Calories 212 Fat 7.1 g Carbs 0.4 g Protein 34.5 g

Seasoned Beef Roast

Preparation Time: 10 Minutes

Cooking Time: 45 Minutes

Servings: 10

Ingredients:

• 3 pounds beef top roast

• One tablespoon olive oil

• Two tablespoons Montreal steak seasoning

Directions:

1. Coat the roast with oil and then rub with the seasoning generously.

2. With kitchen twines, tie the roast to keep it compact. Arrange the roast onto the cooking tray.

3. Select "Air Fry" and then alter the temperature to 360 degrees F. Set the timer for 45 minutes and press the "Start."

4. If the display shows "Add Food," insert the cooking tray in the center position.

5. When the display shows "Turn Food," do nothing.

6. When cooking time is complete, take away the tray from Vortex.

7.   Place the roast onto a platter for about 10 minutes before slicing.

8.   With a sharp knife, cut the roast into desired sized slices and serve.

Nutrition: Calories 269 Fat 9.9 g Carbs 0 g Fiber 0 g

SNACKS

Sweet Potato Tater Tots

Preparation Time: 10 Minutes

Cooking Time: 23 Minutes

Servings: 4

Ingredients:

• 2 sweet potatoes, peeled

• 1/2 tsp. Cajun seasoning

• Olive oil cooking spray

• Sea salt to taste

Directions:

1. Boil sweet potatoes in water for 15 minutes over medium-high heat.

2. Drain the sweet potatoes then allow them to cool.

3. Peel the boiled sweet potatoes and return them to the bowl.

4. Mash the potatoes and stir in salt and Cajun seasoning. Mix well and make small tater tots out of it.

5.   Place the tater tots in the Dutch oven basket and spray them with cooking oil. Set the Dutch oven basket inside the Dutch oven toaster oven and close the lid. Select the Air Fry mode at 400°F temperature for 8 minutes. Flip the tater tots and continue cooking for another 8 minutes.

6.   Serve fresh.

Nutrition: Calories: 184 Cal Protein: 9 g Carbs: 43 g Fat: 17 g

DESSERTS

Shrimp Bacon Bites

Preparation Time: 8 to 10 Minutes

Cooking Time: 8 Minutes

Servings: 8 to 10

Ingredients:

- 1/2 teaspoon red pepper flakes, crushed

- 1 tablespoon salt

- 1 teaspoon chili powder

- 1 ¼ pounds shrimp, peeled and deveined

- 1 teaspoon paprika

- 1/2 teaspoon black pepper, ground

- 1 tablespoon shallot powder

- 1/4 teaspoon cumin powder

- 1 ¼ pounds thin bacon slices

Directions:

1.   Place your dutch ovenon a flat kitchen surface; plug it and turn it on. Set temperature to 360 degrees F and let it preheat for 4-5 minutes.

2. Take out the air-frying basket and gently coat it using a cooking oil or spray.

3. In a bowl of medium size, thoroughly mix the shrimp and seasoning until they are coated well.

4. Now wrap a slice of bacon around the shrimps; secure them with a toothpick and refrigerate for 30 minutes.

5. Add the shrimps to the basket. Push the air-frying basket in the air fryer. Cook for 8 minutes.

6. Slide out the basket; serve with cocktail sticks or your choice of dip (optional).

Nutrition: Calories – 374 Fat – 28.2g Carbohydrates – 2g Fiber – 0g Protein – 34.3g

Healthy Blueberry Muffins

Preparation Time: 10 Minutes

Cooking Time: 10 Minutes

Servings: 8 to 10

Ingredients:

- 2 teaspoons vanilla extract
- 1 cup blueberries
- ½ teaspoon salt
- 1 cup yogurt
- 1 ½ cups cake flour
- ½ cup sugar
- 2 teaspoons baking powder
- 1/3 cup vegetable oil
- 1 egg

Directions:

1. Place your dutch ovenon a flat kitchen surface; plug it and turn it on. Set temperature to 355 degrees F and let it preheat for 4-5 minutes.

2. Take 10 muffin molds and gently coat them using a cooking oil or spray.

3.   In a bowl of medium size, thoroughly mix the flour, sugar, baking powder and salt.

4.   In a bowl of medium size, thoroughly mix the yogurt, oil, egg and vanilla extract. Mix both bowl mixtures. Add the chocolate chips.

5.   Add the mixture into prepared muffin molds evenly.

6.   Add the molds in the basket. Push the air-frying basket in the air fryer. Cook for 10 minutes.

7.   Slide out the basket; serve warm!

Nutrition: Calories - 214 Fat – 8g Carbohydrates – 32g Fiber – 1g Protein – 4g

CAST IRON

BREAKFAST

Roasted Root Vegetables

Preparation Time: 15 minutes

Cooking Time: 45 minutes

Servings: 6

Ingredients:

- 1 large red onion, peeled
- 1 bunch of red beets, trimmed, peeled
- 1 large yam, peeled
- 1 bunch of golden beets, trimmed, peeled
- 1 large parsnips, peeled
- 1 butternut squash, peeled
- 1 large carrot, peeled
- 6 garlic cloves, peeled
- 3 tablespoons thyme leaves
- Salt as needed
- 1 cinnamon stick
- Ground black pepper as needed
- 3 tablespoons olive oil

- 2 tablespoons honey

Directions:

1. Switch on the Pellet grill, fill the grill hopper with hickory flavored wood pellets, power the grill on by using the control panel, select 'smoke' on the temperature dial, or set the temperature to 450 degrees F and let it preheat for a minimum of 15 minutes.

2. Meanwhile, cut all the vegetables into ½-inch pieces, place them in a large bowl, add garlic, thyme, and cinnamon, drizzle with oil and toss until mixed.

3. Take a large cookie sheet, line it with foil, spread with vegetables, and then season with salt and black pepper.

4. When the grill has preheated, open the lid, place prepared cookie sheet on the grill grate, shut the grill and smoke for 45 minutes until tender.

5. When done, transfer vegetables to a dish, drizzle with honey, and then serve.

Nutrition: Calories: 164 Cal Fat: 4 g Carbs: 31.7 g Protein: 2.7 g Fiber: 6.4 g

Vegetable Skewers

Preparation Time: 10 minutes

Cooking Time: 20 minutes

Servings: 4

Ingredients:

- 2 cups whole white mushrooms

- 2 large yellow squash, peeled, chopped

- 1 cup chopped pineapple

- 1 cup chopped red pepper

- 1 cup halved strawberries

- 2 large zucchini, chopped

For the Dressing:

- 2 lemons, juiced

- ½ teaspoon ground black pepper

- 1/2 teaspoon sea salt

- 1 teaspoon red chili powder

- 1 tablespoon maple syrup

- 1 tablespoon orange zest

- 2 tablespoons apple cider vinegar

- 1/4 cup olive oil

Directions:

1. Switch on the Pellet grill, fill the grill hopper with flavored wood pellets, power the grill on by using the control panel, select 'smoke' on the temperature dial, or set the temperature to 450 degrees F and let it preheat for a minimum of 5 minutes.

2. Meanwhile, prepared thread vegetables and fruits on skewers alternately and then brush skewers with oil.

3. When the grill has preheated, open the lid, place vegetable skewers on the grill grate, shut the grill, and smoke for 20 minutes until tender and lightly charred.

4. Meanwhile, prepare the dressing and for this, take a small bowl, place all of its ingredients in it and then whisk until combined.

5. When done, transfer skewers to a dish, top with prepared dressing and then serve.

Nutrition: Calories: 130 Cal Fat: 2 g Carbs: 20 g Protein: 2 g Fiber: 0.3 g Vegetable Recipes

LUNCH

Smoked Whole Duck

Preparation Time: 15 minutes

Cooking Time: 2 hours 30 minutes

Servings: 4

Ingredients:

- 2 Tablespoons of baking soda

- 1 Tablespoon of Chinese five spices

- 1 Thawed duck

- 1 Granny smith cored and diced apple

- 1 Quartered sliced orange

- 2 Tablespoons of chicken seasoning, divided

Directions:

1.	Start by washing the duck under cool running water from the inside and out; then pat the meat dry with clean paper towels

2.	Combine the Chicken seasoning and the Chinese Five spice; then combine with the baking soda for extra crispy skin

3.   Season the duck from the inside and out

4.   Tuck the apple and the orange and apple slices into the cavity.

5.   Turn your Wood Pellet Smoker Grill to smoke model; then let the fire catch and set it to about 300°F to preheat

6.   Place the duck on the grill grate or in a pan. Roast for about 2 ½ hours at a temperature of about 160°F

7.   Place the foil loosely on top of the duck and let rest for about 15 minutes.

8.   Serve and enjoy your delicious dish!

Nutrition: Amount per 184 g= 1 serving(s)Energy (calories): 310 kcal Protein: 23.8 g Fat: 20.62 g Carbohydrates: 5.92 g

Smoked Venison

Preparation Time: 10 minutes

Cooking Time: 2 hours

Servings: 4

Ingredients

- 1 lb. of venison tenderloin
- ¼ Cup of lemon juice
- ¼ Cup of olive oil
- 5 Minced garlic cloves
- 1 tsp. of salt
- 1 tsp. of ground black pepper

Directions:

1. Start by putting the whole venison tenderloin in a zip-style bag or a large bowl.

2. Add the lemon juice, the olive oil, the garlic, the salt, and the pepper into a food processor

3. Process your ingredients until they are very well incorporated

4. Pour the marinade on top of the venison; then massage it in very well

5.   Refrigerate and let marinate for about 4 hours or an overnight

6.   When you are ready to cook, just remove your marinade's venison and rinse it off very well.

7.   Pat the meat dry and let it come to room temperature for about 30 minutes before cooking it

8.   In the meantime, preheat your smoker to a temperature of about 225°F

9.   Smoke the tenderloin for about 2 hours

10.   Let the meat rest for about 10 minutes before slicing it

11.   Top with black pepper; then serve and enjoy your dish!

Nutrition: Amount per 159 g= 1 serving(s) Energy (calories): 302 kcal Protein: 34.42 g Fat: 16.24 g Carbohydrates: 3.36 g

DINNER

Baked Cornbread with Honey Butter

Preparation Time: 10 minutes

Cooking Time: 35 to 45 minutes

Servings 6

Ingredients:

- 4 ears whole corn
- 1 cup all-purpose flour
- 1 cup cornmeal
- 2/3 cup white sugar
- 1½ teaspoons baking powder
- ½ teaspoon baking soda
- ½ teaspoon salt
- 1 cup buttermilk
- ½ cup butter, softened
- 2 eggs
- ½ cup butter, softened
- ¼ cup honey

Directions:

1.   When ready to cook, set Traeger temperature to High and preheat, lid closed for 15 minutes.

2.   Peel back the outer layer of the corn husk, keeping it attached to the cob. Remove the silk from the corn and place the husk back into place. Soak the corn in cold water for 10 minutes.

3.   Place the corn directly on the grill grate and cook for 15 to 20 minutes, or until the kernels are tender, stirring occasionally. Remove from the grill and set aside.

4.   In a large bowl, stir together the flour, cornmeal, sugar, baking powder, baking soda and salt.

5.   In a separate bowl, whisk together the buttermilk, butter, and eggs. Pour the wet mixture into the cornmeal mixture and fold together until there are no dry spots. Pour the batter into a greased baking dish.

6.   Cut the kernels from the corn and sprinkle over the top of the batter, pressing the kernels down with a spoon to submerge.

7.   Turn Traeger temperature down to 350 F (177 C). Place the baking dish on the grill. Bake for about 20 to 25 minutes,

or until the top is golden brown and a toothpick inserted into the middle of the cornbread comes out clean.

8.   Remove the cornbread from the grill and let cool for 10 minutes before serving.

9.   To make the honey butter, mix the butter and honey until combined. Serve the cornbread with the honey butter.

Nutrition: Calories: 82 Carbs: 22g Fat: 0g Protein: 2g

Quick Yeast Dinner Rolls

Preparation Time: 5 minutes

Cooking Time: 30 minutes

Servings 8

Ingredients:

- 2 tablespoons yeast, quick rise

- 1 cup water, lukewarm

- 3 cups flour

- ¼ cup sugar

- 1 teaspoon salt

- ¼ cup unsalted butter, softened

- 1 egg

- Cooking spray, as needed

- 1 egg, for egg wash

Directions:

1.   Combine the yeast and warm water in a small bowl to activate the yeast. Let sit for about 5 to 10 minutes, or until foamy.

2.   Combine the flour, sugar, and salt in the bowl of a stand mixer fitted with the dough hook. Pour the water and yeast

into the dry ingredients with the machine running on low speed.

3.   Add the butter and egg and mix for 10 minutes, gradually increasing the speed from low to high.

4.   Form the dough into a ball and place in a buttered bowl. Cover with a cloth and let the dough rise for approximately 40 minutes.

5.   Transfer the risen dough to a lightly floured work surface and divide into 8 pieces, forming a ball with each.

6.   Lightly spritz a cast iron pan with cooking spray and arrange the balls in the pan. Cover with a cloth and let rise for 20 minutes.

7.   When ready to cook, set Traeger temperature to 375 F (191 C) and preheat, lid closed for 15 minutes.

8.   Brush the rolls with the egg wash. Place the pan on the grill and bake for 30 minutes, or until lightly browned.

9.   Remove from the grill. Serve hot.

Nutrition: Calories: 390 Carbs: 8g Fat: 31g Protein: 20g

SNACKS

Grilled Brussels Sprouts

Preparation Time: 15 Minutes

Cooking Time: 20 Minutes

Servings: 8

Ingredients

- 1/2 lb. bacon, grease reserved

- 1 lb. Brussels Sprouts

- 1/2 tbsp pepper

- 1/2 tbsp salt

Directions:

1. Cook bacon until crispy on a stovetop, reserve its grease then chop into small pieces.

2. Meanwhile, wash the Brussels sprouts, trim off the dry end, and remove dried leaves if any. Half them and set aside.

3. Place 1/4 cup reserved grease in a pan, cast-iron, over medium-high heat.

4. Season the Brussels sprouts with pepper and salt.

5.   Brown the sprouts on the pan with the cut side down

for about 3-4 minutes.

6.   In the meantime, preheat your pellet grill to 350-375oF.

7.   Place bacon pieces and browned sprouts into your grill-

safe pan.

8.   Cook for about 20 minutes.

9.   Serve immediately.

Nutrition: Calories 153, Total fat 10g, Saturated fat 3g, Total

Carbs 5g, Net Carbs 3g, Protein 11g, Sugars 1g, Fiber 2g,

Sodium 622mg, Potassium 497mg

Wood Pellet Spicy Brisket

Preparation Time: 20 Minutes

Cooking Time: 9 Hours

Servings: 10

Ingredients

- 2 tbsp garlic powder

- 2 tbsp onion powder

- 2 tbsp paprika

- 2 tbsp chili powder

- 1/3 cup salt

- 1/3 cup black pepper

- 12 lb. whole packer brisket, trimmed

- 1-1/2 cup beef broth

Directions:

1.   Set your wood pellet temperature to 225°F. Let preheat for 15 minutes with the lid closed.

2.   Meanwhile, mix garlic, onion, paprika, chili, salt, and pepper in a mixing bowl.

3.   the brisket generously on all sides.

4.   Place the meat on the grill with the fat side down and let it cool until the internal temperature reaches 160°F.

5.   Remove the meat from the grill and double wrap it with foil. Return it to the grill and cook until the internal temperature reaches 204°F.

6.   Remove from grill, unwrap the brisket and let rest for 15 minutes.

7.   Slice and serve.

Nutrition: Calories 270, Total fat 20g, Saturated fat 8g, Total Carbs 3g, Net Carbs 3g, Protein 20g, Sugar 1g, Fiber 0g, Sodium: 1220mg

DESSERTS

Deep Fried Prawns

Preparation Time: 20 Minutes

Cooking Time: 15 Minutes

Servings: 6

Ingredients:

- 12 prawns

- Two eggs

- Flour to taste

- Breadcrumbs

- 1 tsp oil

Directions:

1.   Remove the head of the prawns and shell carefully.

2.   Pass the prawns first in the flour, then in the beaten egg, and then in the breadcrumbs.

3.   Preheat the cast iron for 1 minute at 1500C.

4.   Add the prawns and cook for 4 minutes. If the prawns are large, it will be necessary to cook six at a time.

5.   Turn the prawns and cook for another 4 minutes.

6.   They should be served with a yogurt or mayonnaise
sauce.

Nutrition: Calories 2385.1 Fat 23 Carbohydrates 52.3g Sugar
0.1g Protein 21.4g

CPSIA information can be obtained
at www.ICGtesting.com
Printed in the USA
BVHW092344170521
607553BV00002B/210

9 781802 412994